Watchman on The Wall...
For Such a Time as This

A compilation of inspiring poetry,
evocative messages
and thought-provoking Pastoral
Words of Wisdom

Dr. G. Gregg Murray

Watchman on the Wall...
For Such a Time as This

Copyright 2009

Printed in the United States of America

ISBN 978-0-9843245-8-3

Published by Parablist Publishing House
P.O. Box 43379
Richmond Heights, OH 44143

Cover Design and Forward by Deborah A. Wright

Table of Contents

Forward

Dr. G. Gregg Murray has a way with words! As a straight shooting Preacher of the Gospel, poet, prolific writer, and messenger of hope, Pastor G. Gregg Murray's words inspire!

Pastor G. Gregg Murray utilizes mediums such as Facebook to reach thousands of people with his God-inspired messages—raw and uncut.

"Watchman On The Wall...for Such A Time As This" is a compilation of "posts" as seen on Dr. Murray's Facebook page. His messages of truth have been known to either incite cyber riots (LOL) or soothe the jagged edge of discouragement.

At other times, Dr. Murray chisels poetic masterpieces that flow with a sensitivity and sensuality that rival passages of the Song of Solomon, in a modern day vernacular..."Brown Sugar".

This book was compiled in an effort to share the words of encouragement and hope as posted on his wall to people far outside of it's reach.

Pastor G. Gregg Murray has a true heart for people. His prayer is that the words of truth herein, engrave themselves upon the walls of our hearts; and that we may develop a closer relationship to God and to our fellowman while sharing a laugh or two along the way!

Deborah A. Wright, CEO
Parablist Publishing House

Introduction

I thank God for the completion of this book. It is my desire that the words written herein incite a righteous movement on the inside of all of those who read it; a movement towards a more intimate relationship with God; and a movement towards enriched and gratifying relationships with our fellow man.

Dedication

This book is dedicated to my beloved children' Shalonda, Gregg, Jr, Moriah, Judayah, Joshua and Jeremiah who accept a father who is always gone too long. To my loving mother, Laura Murray, who raised me and nurtured me from a boy of flesh to a man of God. To my loving Church family, The New Salem Missionary Baptist Church of Syracuse, NY, all of whom I love so dearly. In memory of my loving sisters, Lorraine and Linda. To my darling sister Kindell, and my needy brother Tony…we are family! And to all of my family and friends around the world. None of me is possible without you. I thank God for you all. May you continue to seek truth and pursue it.

Pastor's Prayer

Lord, you have given me a great blessing

and an awesome responsibility.

Help me to be worthy.

Grant me **ABILITY** to counsel wisely and well.

STRENGTH to practice what I preach.

COURAGE to walk in your truth.

GRACE to help lead others to you.

Let everything I do, be done in your name.

AMEN

Sweet 16
(Moriah turns 16)

A little girl no more... outwardly growing and inwardly knowing. coming into womanhood, standing at the threshold.

God's creation moving steadily along into mature beauty. She's still my little girl...and I'm still her daddy.

Predestined to be every woman. Confirming the fore knowledge of God that you are wonderfully and fearfully made.

No longer a little girl but not quite a full woman... ever becoming you.

Looking at the world differently and the world looking at you differently.

Wisdom becoming more shapely. You are my sweet 16, you are my daughter...

She's me...I want to protect her always... I have to loosen my daddy hugs a little now and let her be...

So God has to take over her heart now... The God I tried so hard to show her.

I will always be here when you need to talk to a man... I will always cherish our special moments together.

As you grow...we grow closer. Though you travel more on your own now.

I trust the God that I tried to show to you.
I know He is in your heart.

That's what truly makes your sweet 16 birthday...
even more sweeter.

I thank God for you my Sweet 16.
Judayah is next!

Change Is Coming

Change is coming soon.
You've been waiting on change for a long time now.
You thought change would never come.
But, change is coming soon.
Get ready for change...get ready to receive it.
Are you making room for the change?
Will you be ready for it when it comes?
Will there be room enough to receive it?
Sometimes change comes like a thief in the night...
no warning.
We pray for change...but sometimes it comes
in ways we don't expect.
We want change...but real change only comes
when we need it...and we act on it.
Change is that real.
There are two changes...
For better...the other for worse.
It all depends on you...
It depends on where inside of you
the desire for change originates.
The real question to ask is…
"is change wanted or needed...
and what am I willing to do to bring change to me?"
There is a difference.
The difference will determine when and where or even if
change will come.
Change can give and change can take away.
God can orchestrate change...but so can satan!
I can feel the winds shifting.
I can see the leaves about to turn colors and fall away...
Making way for the new..."good to bad...or bad to good"
Summer to winter...or winter to summer!
Change is coming...I can smell it!

Brown Sugar

I love my Brown Sugar!
Ain't anything like it...

It's sweet in a brown sort of way.
It has colorful attitude.

Don't get me wrong...white sugar has it's place...
But ain't anything like this "Brown Sugar."

It can sweeten the most bitter situations.
It can color the most dull portrait.

The first sweetener was this Brown Sugar.
God saw fit that all other sugar would find their roots in
this Brown Sugar.

Brown Sugar is the mother of all sweetness...
Brown Sugar is not to be compared...it cannot be!

Sway those hips and lips...and pray with me.
Walk that brown sugar walk…and talk that brown sugar
talk to my heart.

Brown Sugar wants to pray with me.
Brown Sugar wants to support and help me.

Brown Sugar want to build me up and praise me.
Brown Sugar wants me to be a man...only her man!

I love me some Brown Sugar.
God saw that my cake was missing
a critical and vital ingredient...

So He reached out of my own man sweetness and pulled
out some Brown Sugar just for me.

It was in it's raw form...and God told me to form that
Brown Sugar, and to breath deeply into her and to make
and bake her into a sweet pastry
in the heated oven of my authentic love.

God brought that Brown Sugar to me and I tasted it which
was actually tasting myself...
and I saw that it was pleasant and good.

God said...Respect your Brown Sugar because there is
none exactly like her.

God said honor your Brown Sugar because she is
fearfully and wonderfully made.

God said love your Brown Sugar because
if you love her...

she will forever sweeten your deepest needs.
Yes...Brown Sugar...You're my sweet wife!

I thank God for my Brown Sugar

Living in the Now

Yesterday is in the past. Tomorrow is in the future. Right "now" is all that there is. If nothing changes "now," nothing will be changed later. It all starts right "now." Are you living in your "was," or your "later," or your "now"? You really don't even own the present moment, for even this belongs to God.

Often we hear people talking about the need to manage time and to set or reset or 're-reset priorities' and so on. I have also been one such person. But, now I know that 'it is not time that needs to be managed, but it is ourselves'. When we know how to manage ourselves, then time, financial, relational and all other managements fall in place almost automatically. We cannot manage ourselves without a clear knowledge of and commitment to 'the purpose of our life'. It is not the priorities that need to be set first, but it is rather 'the purpose of our life' that needs to be fixed firmly in our minds and hearts. That is why we are focusing our attention on "Living in the Now," (in an important sense, living a 'Purpose Driven Life').

We should have a past and should cherish our past. At the same time, only the silliest nostalgia freak wants to live in the past.

Then, what about the future? Once again, we should anticipate a future and we should cherish the future that we anticipate. Not to anticipate a future is to live for instant gratification in the present -- and we have already noted the perils of that immaturity.

At the same time, even as we anticipate our future and cherish it we must not live for the future. People who live for the future are investing everything in the future, with the result that the present is worthless. People who live for the future are counting on so very much twenty-five years from now that the present counts for nothing. People who assume that waves of happiness are going to flood them in fifteen years are plainly joyless today.

To live in the past is to bury oneself in a past that never was -- and therein render the present insignificant. To live for the future is to fantasize about a future that is never going to be -- and therein render the present insignificant.

Then the only thing to do is cherish both past and future yet live in the present; in fact, live in the present alone.

Life so often seems to be a delicate balance between accepting what is and changing what ought not to be. It is a challenge of perspective; connecting past experience and future hope into a present moment. How do you find the balance?

Well, the more I give myself permission to live in the moment and enjoy it without feeling guilty, the better I feel about the quality of my life. There is one thing we can do, and the happiest people are those who can do it to the limit of their ability. We can be completely present. We can be all here. We can give all our attention to the opportunity before us. Above all, live in the present moment and God will give you all the grace you need.

"Therefore do not worry about tomorrow, for tomorrow will worry about itself. Each day has enough troubles of its own." Matthew 6:24

O God, Grant me the serenity to accept the things I cannot change, The courage to change the things I can, And the wisdom to know the difference.

Living one day at a time, enjoying one moment at a time, accepting hardships as the pathway to peace. Taking, as He did, this sinful world as it is, not as I would have it. Trusting that He will make all things right if I surrender to His will; that I may be reasonably happy in this world and supremely happy with Him forever. Amen.

Who Is Your Covering?

There is a popular teaching coming from the pulpits of many apostate churches today, which claims that Christians must have a "spiritual covering". This teaching as it is presented in today's church is a far cry from what Paul taught in I Corinthians 11.

The covering taught by most pastors today is the idea that a Christian must be a member of a church and must be spiritually submitted to a particular pastor. Many will tell you that if you are not submitted to a church hierarchy you are out of the will of God and are under the influence of satan. All of this is evidence of the Nicolaitan error Jesus spoke of in Revelation 2:6

"But, I would have you know, that the head of every man is Christ; and the head of the woman is the man; and the head of Christ is God." I Cor. 11:3

Notice that Paul does not say the head of every man is his pastor, or an apostle, or any other church official. The head of every man is Christ. Period!

Every man praying or prophesying, having his head covered, dishonoureth his head. But, every woman that prayeth or prophesieth with her head uncovered dishonoureth her head: for that is even all one as if she were shaven. I Cor. 11:4-5

Paul is not talking here about wearing a hat or a prayer shawl or the length of one's hair. What he is saying is this. Every man who covers his head by submitting himself to another man dishonors his true head, which is

Christ. And, any woman who worships without the covering of her husband dishonors her husband.

There is no higher authority in the body of Christ than the individual believer. All Christians are seen by God as kings and priests. All are called saints. All who do the will of God are counted as sons of God. Every man will be accountable by himself for his own actions or inactions vis-à-vis his relationship with the Lord Jesus Christ. Your pastor or apostle to whom you have submitted yourself will not be there to speak for you.

Some will point to Hebrews 13:17 as a reason we should spiritually submit to men.

Obey them that have the rule over you, and submit yourselves: for they watch for your souls, as they that must give account, that they may do it with joy, and not with grief: for that is unprofitable for you. Heb 13:17

The Greek word which is translated them that have the rule is the word hegeomai {hayg-eh'-om-ahee} which means to lead or to go before. Our misunderstanding of this principle stems from our conformity to the world and the way leadership is exercised in this earthly realm.

But, Jesus called them unto him, and said, "Ye know that the princes of the Gentiles exercise dominion over them, and they that are great exercise authority upon them. But, it shall not be so among you: but whosoever will be great among you, let him be your minister; And whosoever will be chief among you, let him be your servant". Matt. 20:25-27

We see here that leadership in the Kingdom of God consists of servanthood. Those who God has called to the five-fold ministry are placed there to be your servant not your master. You are not called to serve them. So, those who have rule over us must be those who give of themselves to see that we are conformed to the image of Christ. What they will give account of is how well they performed their role as servant.

Unfortunately, just as Paul prophesied in Acts 20:29, grievous wolves have entered into the church intent on drawing away disciples unto themselves. One way they do this is to intimidate people into following them. It is amazing the amount of fear and guilt these supposed shepherds put on the unsuspecting sheep.

I heard one pastor tell his congregation that all their prosperity is due to his faith. He talks often about people who have left his church and are now poor and sick. The people who sit under him are afraid to leave.

I listened once to a well known Televangelist tell a congregation that God put them under their pastor and that if they ever left that pastor they were in rebellion to God. People were whoopin and hollerin and cheering him on. He went on and on getting all worked up until he finally said; "I know you have Jesus but Jesus is not enough!"

A stunned silence filled the auditorium. This Televangelist got a funny look on his face as if he himself was surprised that those words had come out of his mouth. After a moment, he composed himself and began to tap dance and back track trying to explain what he really meant. But, I knew what he meant. Jesus said out of the abundance of the heart the mouth speaks (Luke 6:45). That was the spirit of antichrist (in place of Christ) talking out of that man's mouth. What is really sad is that not one person got up and left. After a couple of awkward minutes they were back whoopin and hollerin for this wolf in sheep's clothing.

I know that there are rebellious people in the body of Christ who refuse to submit to any authority. I have no problem submitting to Godly authority when I see it. I must say that Godly authority is a rare thing in the church today but it does exist.

The people to whom you should submit are those who have gone before you. Those who know more than you do. No single individual, be it pastor, teacher, apostle prophet, or evangelist has all the answers for every situation you will face in life. We are all only parts of the body. No single person is the complete body except Christ. That is why you should submit to Him. If Christ leads you to an individual for a time of instruction then sit and learn from that person. But, understand that it is the gift in them to which Christ has led you, not the person.

So, the lesson here is this--submit yourself to Christ. He is your head. Allow him to be your teacher. If he sends you to a person for a season fine, learn from that servant . But, you should never allow that person to exercise rulership over you in the earthly sense. If you are born again and filled with the Holy Ghost, you are perfectly capable of hearing from God yourself. You are perfectly capable of understanding the Bible yourself. You are perfectly capable of obeying God yourself.

Lord...Are You Pleased With Me?

Are you pleased with my walk, Lord?
Do you like the fact that when I stumble,
I lean on you a little more?

Even when I take mis-steps,
you are always there to gently
yet firmly guide me back on track.

Sometimes my steps take me to places that are dark,
but, you are always a lamp for my feet,
and a light for my path.

Are you pleased with my talk, Lord?
Do you like the fact that I want my word to be your Word?
You constantly teach me how to teach my mouth.

You allow the words of my mouth
and the meditations of my heart
to be acceptable in your sight.

Sometimes, my mouth is full of your Word
yet, I don't speak it like I should,
but your Holy Spirit is always there
to strengthen my heart

so that the words will flow so sweetly
and gently from my heart,
to my mouth, and off of my lips
on to the ears of your creation.

Are you pleased with my mind, Lord?
Do you like the fact that I meditate on your Word daily,
and I have learned to delight myself in your commands?

Do you like my study habits?
I try my best not to allow certain spirits to come into view.
Because I know what I see,
affects how I think.

I try my best not to expose my ears to any and every thing.
because I know what I hear, affects how I think.
I desire the mind of Christ.

You give me the desires of my heart.
Please continue to help me bring
my every thought and every imagination
under your holy and righteous captivity
so that I can be more like you.

Are you pleased with my choices, Lord?
Do you like the fact that I consult with you
before I make choices now.

Help me to make the choices that I make
be the choices you have made for me.
I'm trying to make more healthier choices for me
and those that I am responsible for.

Thank you for giving me time to evaluate
and receive your information before I choose.
I choose you today,
Your ways, your time...your will!

I understand that I am a product of my choices!
Are you pleased with my fruit, Lord?
Do you like the fact that I am serious about the fruit I bear.
I understand now, that I am known by the fruit I produce.

I want to produce much good fruit,
so I make sure I sow according to your Word,

thereby reaping according to your Word.

I make sure that my ground remains fertile
and receptive to the Seed of your Word.
I hope that when you taste my fruit
You will notice the sincerity of my heart
to please you in all my ways.

I want my fruit to harvest in due season.
Strengthen me as a true Laborer in your vineyard.
Are you pleased with me, Lord?
Are you pleased with my worship?
Are you pleased with my praise?
Are you pleased with my prayer?
Are you pleased with my imperfection?
Are you pleased to call me your child?

If there is anything in me that is not pleasing to You...
please continue to work on me and help me to stand.
Because even though I know
I don't always please you...
You know I always want to please you.
Thank you for keeping me, Lord!

Why Are You So Afraid?

I am compelled to write something about FEAR. Fear comes from the enemy of the church. For God hath not given us the spirit of fear; but of power, and of love, and of a sound mind.

Many in the church today are living in fear of man. This is one of the biggest issues facing the church today...FEAR!

It seems as though everyone wants to be liked by all men, and no one wants to offend anyone anymore. Well...woe unto you, when all men shall speak well of you! for so did their fathers to the false prophets.

The crown is fallen from our head: woe unto us, that we have feared man, rather than feared God!

The LORD is my light and my salvation; whom shall I fear? The LORD is the strength of my life; of whom shall I be afraid?

Only he who can say, "The Lord is the strength of my life" can say, "Of whom shall I be afraid?" We stand at the crossroads between fear of others and fear of God. The road leading to the fear of man may be expressed in terms of favoritism, wanting others to think well of you, fearing exposure by them, or being overwhelmed by their perceived physical power. When these fears are not combated with the fear of the Lord, the consequences can be devastating. But, when God is given his rightful place in our lives, old bonds can be shattered...Of whom shall I be afraid? One with God is a majority.

When the wicked, even mine enemies and my foes, came upon me to eat up my flesh, they stumbled and fell. Though an host should encamp against me, my heart shall not fear: though war should rise against me, in this will I be confident. One thing have I desired of the LORD, that will I seek after; that I may dwell in the house of the LORD all the days of my life, to behold the beauty of the LORD, and to enquire in his temple.

We fear men so much, because we fear God so little. One fear cures another. When man's terror scares you, turn your thoughts to the wrath of God. However, you put it, the fear of man can be summarized this way: We replace God with people. Instead of a Biblically guided fear of the Lord, we fear others.

The "fear of man" goes by other names. When we are in our teens, it is called "peer pressure." When we are older, it is called "people-pleasing." Recently, it has been called "codependency." With these labels in mind, we can spot the fear of man everywhere. We fear people because they can expose and humiliate us. We fear people because they can reject, ridicule, or despise us. We fear people because they can attack, oppress, or threaten us. These three reasons have one thing in common: they see people as "bigger" (that is, more powerful and significant) than God, and, out of the fear that is created in us, we give other people the power and right to tell us what to feel, think, and do.

What is the result of people-idolatry? As in all idolatry, the idol we choose to worship soon owns us. The object we fear overcomes us. Although insignificant in itself, the idol becomes huge and rules us. It tells us how to think, what to feel, and how to act. It tells us what to wear, it tells us to laugh at the dirty joke, and it tells us to be frightened to death that we might have to get up in front of a group and say something. The whole strategy backfires. We never expect that using people to meet our desires, leaves us enslaved to them. We are more concerned about looking stupid (a fear of people) than we are about acting sinfully (fear of the Lord).

Understanding Bible prophecy encourages in two unique ways. First, it serves as a reminder that God controls history. When, you read from the pages of Scripture how He keeps His promises, your faith is strengthened. By reflecting on the fulfilled promises of the past, you can find great comfort as you look toward the future. Second, understanding God's promises for the future provides a solid foundation to which you can anchor your hope—a sturdy shield with which you can deflect your doubts and fears about tomorrow...When you reflect on God's plans and promises for you and for the world, you can face the future without fear.

In God I will praise his Word, in God I have put my trust; I will not fear what flesh can do unto me. And, fear not them which kill the body, but are not able to kill the soul: but rather fear him which is able to destroy both soul and body in hell. So that we may boldly say, "The Lord is my helper, and I will not fear what man shall do unto me." There is no fear in love; but perfect love casteth out fear: because fear hath torment. He that feareth is not made perfect in love. If the Lord be with us, we have no cause of fear. His eye is upon us, His arm over us, His ear open to our prayer – His grace sufficient, His promise unchangeable.

Jesus replied, "You of little faith, why are you so afraid?" Then he got up and rebuked the winds and the waves, and it was completely calm.

Fear knocked at the door. Faith answered. Fear fled... It's time for the church to come out of the shell that we have allowed the "fear of man" to place us in.

A Word About Loneliness

I feel prompted by the Holy Spirit to write something about loneliness. There are too many people in the world today suffering from a spirit of "loneliness."

The first negative judgment we find in the Word of God is a judgment on loneliness. God said, "It is not good for man to be alone."

Like Elijah, Jeremiah, Jesus, or Paul, you may be experiencing intense loneliness. A person does not have to be single to be lonely. You can be married and living with your spouse. In fact, your loneliness may be exaggerated because of feeling trapped in a marriage with a person who is withdrawn and aloof. Elijah and Jeremiah were overwhelmed with their loneliness. Jesus and Paul were not. The difference is Elijah and Jeremiah felt sorry for themselves while Jesus and Paul sought refuge in God.

The subject of this chapter is to address loneliness. It is really amazing in a world of over 6 billion people that loneliness can be so pandemic. I want to deal with some symptoms and causes of loneliness. Loneliness is real and is not imagined as it is widespread in the Church. It is not peculiar to only one group.
Loneliness affects our:

1. Attitudes;

2. Outlook on life;

3. Motivations;

4. Relationships;

5. Spirituality.

Our help can only come from the Word of God, the only foundation that a Christian can grasp healing truth from.

A lonely person attempts to fill voids in their life with material goods. There is a belief that loneliness will flee if they have more material things, to satisfy the flow of loneliness. This leads to consistent lifestyle of buying and selling which may cause a person to incur much debt to keep up with others. Materialism does not deliver a person from the bondage of loneliness, instead it projects them into another form of bondage.

A lonely person will turn some appliance on whenever they enter a room, even if it is not conducive to whatever they are planning, a radio, TV, stereo, or something just to break the spell of quietness. Quietness can be a thing of great beauty but to a lonely person it is like a coffin.

There are many circumstances in which loneliness may be experienced. You may feel lonely when:

1. Guilt causes you to feel separated from God Psalms 25:16, from other men – Genesis 27:1-29; 32:24; 33:1-17.

2. You feel rejected, abandoned, deserted by others John16:32; 2 Tim. 4:16, 17.

3. You are voluntarily or forcefully removed from a safe, secure environment.
4. You experience the "let down" after a spiritual victory. I Kings 19:10, 14.

5. Previous successes or popularity have subsided.

6. You have suffered a defeat.

7. You are too busy chasing "success" to relate to others.

8. You are "burned out" after having tried to achieve by self-effort – John 8:29.

9. You are separated from the group by leadership responsibilities, "lonely at the top" Num. 11:14, 17; Deut. 1:9, 12; Matt 26:38-40.

10. You have suffered the loss of a loved one by death or divorce.

11. You are fearful and timid – I John 4:18.

12. You feel inferior, unworthy, self-condemnation, insecure.

13. You are physically removed or separated from those you know and love.

14. Others reject or ostracize you for being different, or for nonconformity.

15. You fail to resolve conflict and misunderstanding; estrangement.

16. You fail to communicate; avoidance; repression; stuff emotions.

17. You have chosen to "stand alone" against

world, sin, religion – Jer. 15:17.

18. Others are not enthused about your interests or project.

19. You don't take the time to enjoy others and have fun together.

20. You have been prejudged, stereotyped, pegged, put in a box.

21. Your particular talents, abilities and personality are not appreciated.

22. You don't fit in—economically, intellectually, politically, religiously, etc.

23. You do not feel connected, bonded or able to relate emotionally or spiritually.

24. Friends only relate on a superficial level; will not get serious and real.

25. You have been excluded from a particular social grouping.

26. You feel like an outsider, the "odd man out."

27. Your present responsibilities (parenting, vocation, etc.) preclude or diminish the development of relationships.

28. You retire from your vocation and no longer relate to colleagues daily.

29. Another person is regarded as your "life," and they can't meet all your needs.

30. You do not feel a sense of oneness, unity and intimacy with your mate.

31. You have refused to receive the love and intimacy of your mate.

32. You have been betrayed by a mate or a friend Gen. 3:12.

33. You alienate others by your verbosity, accusations, insensitive comments.

34. You alienate others by using them in competitive or economic success.

35. You alienate others by criticism, negativism, sarcasm, pessimism, hostility, cruelty.

36. You alienate others by your selfishness, egotism, or spiritual pride.

37. You make work, projects, things, possessions more important than people.

38. You feel you cannot perform up to expectations.

39. Others are too preoccupied with their concerns to relate with you.

40. Crisis arises and no one offers to listen or assist.

41. You feel left behind by a fast-paced technological society.

42. Children grow up, go to school, leave home.

43. Isolated due to injury; secluded or ignored due to age (Ps. 71:9, 18).

The key to breaking the loneliness grip on you is found in Matthew 7:7: "Ask, and it shall be given you; seek, and ye shall find; knock, and it shall be opened unto you:

ASK for boldness of spirit to reach out. Ask for open doors of opportunity. Ask for a close Christian friend (Prayer Partner). Ask for ways to broaden your friendship base with like-minded people. Ask for spiritual guidance on how to be more "neighborly".

SEEK opportunities in your realm of ability. There are plenty of things to do with your gifts and talents. You need to do some research where you can find open doors. If you are serious about reclaiming your Christian life, talk to your pastor, I am sure he will have work for you around the church. The key is to be available and ready.

KNOCK on the doors of opportunity. When you find someplace you believe you would fit in, go for it. Do not fear because satan has no problem exchanging gifts. He will be glad to exchange your loneliness for fear. God will have a place of service for you (it is probably waiting for you right now) but you must trust Him to place you in His time and place. Also support groups, (with people with common issues as you), are a great place to meet new people.

34

Did you notice the cure for loneliness? It is not a great mystery and does not even require in-depth counseling but it does involve guidance. Loneliness is cured by a voluntary desire to reclaim your life for Christ and serve Him as you are commanded to. You may not have caused your loneliness but may have nurtured it. God is right there to help you and pick you up. You see loneliness is the only prison where you pass a judgment, sentence yourself, and then carry out the sentence in your own prison.

Remember, loneliness can lead to depression and self-pity. Loneliness can harm your health. If you are lonely, you do not have to stay lonely. Find strength. Find hope. Decide today that you are going to get rid of this loneliness once and for all. As long as you have Christ in your life, you are never really alone.

Does Love Still Live Here?

I hear Jesus saying...can you show me some love?
I Corinthians 13

Love. "If I speak in the tongues of men and of angels, but have not love, I am only a resounding gong or a clanging cymbal. If I have the gift of prophecy and can fathom all mysteries and all knowledge, and if I have a faith that can move mountains, but have not love, I am nothing. If I give all I possess to the poor and surrender my body to the flames, but have not love, I gain nothing.

Love is patient. Love is kind. It does not envy, it does not boast, it is not proud. It is not rude, it is not self-seeking, it is not easily angered, it keeps no record of wrongs. Love does not delight in evil but rejoices with the truth. It always protects, always trusts, always hopes, always perseveres.

Love never fails. But, where there are prophecies, they will cease; where there are tongues, they will be stilled; where there is knowledge, it will pass away. For we know in part and we prophesy in part, but when perfection comes, the imperfect disappears. When I was a child, I talked like a child, I thought like a child, I reasoned like a child. When I became a man, I put childish ways behind me. Now we see but a poor reflection as in a mirror; then we shall see face-to-face. Now I know in part; then I shall know fully, even as I am fully known."

And, now these three remain: faith, hope and love. But, the greatest of these is love. Love is the overflow of joy in God! It is not duty for duty's sake, or right for right's sake. It is not a resolute abandoning of one's own good with a view solely to the good of the other person. It is first a deeply satisfying experience of the fullness of God's grace, and then a doubly satisfying experience of sharing that grace with another person.

According to the world, we love in order to be loved. According to the Word, we love because God first loved us. Whereas the world falls in love, God's people are established in love. The love that we possess, however, is not a fleeting whim that comes and goes with every mood and circumstance; rather, it is a love that is beyond ourselves. Our love, true love, has meaning, meaning that cannot be stripped away by any thing, anyone, or any feeling. Our love cannot be shaken because it is grounded not in self but in sacrifice.

Love is giving – giving of oneself to another. It is not getting, as the world says today. It is not feeling and desire; it is not something over which one has no control. It is something that we do for another. No one loves in the abstract. Love is an attitude that issues forth in something that actually, tangibly happens.

When love is felt, the message is heard.
God is Love.

A Saved Sinner

The Christian life is a war, and the fiercest battles are those that rage within the heart of every believer. The new birth radically and permanently changes a person's sinful nature, but it does not immediately liberate that nature for all of the remnants of sin. Birth is followed by growth, and that growth involves warfare.

The flesh hates everything about God. Since it resists everything about God, it resists every way we try to taste Him and know Him and love Him. And, the more something enables us to find God and feast on Him, the more violently the flesh fights against it. It takes its battle to every quarter of the soul: When the mind wants to know God, the flesh imposes ignorance, darkness, error and trivial thoughts. The will can not move toward God without feeling the weight of stubbornness holding it back. And, the affections, longing to long for God, are constantly fighting the infection of sensuality or the disease of indifference.

Nothing is easier than sin. There is a reason why the enemy makes it so easy to sin.

Although sin should no longer rule us, we still are naturally sinful. God considers us righteous and credits us with the spotless record of Christ, but we still do sin. In fact, the battle with our indwelling sin starts at our conversion. Through justification, we are declared righteous, and it is at this point that our sanctification – our growing in holiness – begins. We are constantly a "work under construction."

But, every last drop of poison is poison; every spark of fire is fire; and the last bit of flesh that remains in the believer is still enmity. When God's grace changes our nature, it does not change the nature of the flesh. It conquers it, weakens it, but only mortally wounds it. By the time Paul wrote Romans, he must have been as Christ-like as anyone can expect to be on this side of heaven, and he surely spent his days putting his flesh to death. Still he cried out for deliverance from this irreconcilable enemy (Rom. 7:24).

The flesh is the old life, the natural life inherited from Adam, with its apparent resources of personality, of ancestry, of commitment, of dedication, and so forth. You can do all kinds of religious things in the flesh. The flesh can preach a sermon. The flesh can sing in the choir. The flesh can serve as an usher. The flesh can lead people to Christ. Did you know that? The flesh can go out and be very zealous in its witnessing and amass a terribly impressive list of people won to Christ, scalps to hang on a belt. The flesh can do these things but it is absolutely nauseating in the eyes of God. It is merely religious activity. There is nothing wrong with what is being done, but what is terribly wrong is the power being relied upon to do it.

If the primary thing keeping you from sinning is the fear of getting caught or the prospect of shame or of being exposed as immoral, you don't stand much of a chance. Oh, these might work for a while. You might find enough strength to resist for the time being. But, the relentless assault of temptation will eventually wear you down and the power of resistance will gradually erode until you give in, tired, frustrated, bitter, angry with God, doubting if a life of obedience will ever bring the satisfaction your soul so deeply craves.

We must learn where our personal weaknesses lie. Once they are identified, we must be ruthless in dealing with them. Earlier generations called this the "mortification of the flesh," that is, pronouncing the death sentence upon sin and putting that sentence into daily effect by killing all that sets itself against God's purpose in our lives.

Prayer is the humble first step in the battle against our indwelling sin. It says, "I am taking sin seriously, I cannot do this on my own, and I need the help of God." When we pray for greater conviction of sin, God will give it to us, and we will be motivated to wage war against it.

As an obedient believer, you are to stand firm in the strength of the Lord, to be sober in spirit, and to remain alert in order to resist the schemes of the devil. However, in all areas of your walk as a believer, you are incapable in your own strength and insufficient in your own resources to overcome the wiles and temptations of Satan. Therefore, you must put on the full armor of God to be an overwhelming conqueror in your continuing spiritual battle.

Any training – physical, mental, or spiritual – is characterized at first by failure. We fail more often than we succeed. But, if we persevere, we gradually see progress till we are succeeding more often than failing. This is true as we seek to put to death particular sins. At first, it seems we are making no progress, so we become discouraged and think, What's the use? I can never overcome that sin. That is exactly what Satan wants us to think. It is at this point that we must exercise perseverance. We keep wanting instant success, but holiness doesn't come that way. Our sinful habits are not broken overnight. Follow-through is required to make any change in our lives, and follow-through requires perseverance.

Knowing God without knowing our own wretchedness makes for pride. Knowing our own wretchedness without knowing God makes for despair.

Knowing Jesus Christ strikes the balance because He shows us both God and our own wretchedness.

O' God deliver me from ME!

God can, God will...Do you believe it?

Jesus Wept

Last night...Jesus came to me, and He was weeping.
You will never know what "divine weeping" is until you
have seen and heard God weep.

His weeping was sorrowfully deep and passionate.
His tears gently rolled down his face to his garment.
His eyes seem tired and painfully hurting.
He just stood at the foot of my bed,
not saying anything...
just weeping and wailing.

I started to weep too...
because I could not bear to hear My Savior, My Lord,
My King...His groans, and His emotions.
I laid on my back weeping and wondering,
and Jesus stood over me weeping and wailing.
We wept together for what seemed like hours.
There are no words to describe weeping with God.
Finally...I developed the strength to ask Jesus...
why He was weeping.

He stopped weeping long enough to tell me these words:
My son, I am weeping because of you.
I have deposited so much into you at Calvary...
and you are wasting what I have given you.
You haven't done all that I have required of you.
You still want to get along with the world.
You still want people to like you, and accept you.

You must understand
that as long as you put anything before Me...
anything (even your feelings)...
you will not be able to have all of Me.
And I want you to have all of Me.

In you, I see such greatness in Me...
In you I see a child who longs for Me,
but you haven't given Me all of you...
And I want all of you,
because that's the only way
you can have ALL of me...

I see you going through so much needless pain...
you are strong and gifted,
but I want to be strong in you.
I want you to have joy always...
and when I see you struggling with useless things...
trying to change this world, and people...
instead of letting Me do it...
I feel for you.

I want to shake you tonight and wake you up...
I created this world...I have victory over this world,
and I have placed that victory within you...
and when you don't walk in total victory...
when you give Satan credit that he doesn't deserve...
It hurts me.

Don't you know...I work ALL things out for your good?
Your sins don't faze me,
because I died for your sins...
before the world was formed
and placed on its foundation...
before your mother had you in her womb.

I knew your sins, and weaknesses...
and when you cry out to me in confessed repentance,
why do you allow the enemy to keep you living beneath
your privilege by causing you to think
of that which I have died for?
Why my child? Why?

You are not walking in total victory...
you have tried to fit in, and that's not what I want of you...
I want you to be sold out for Me,
not a religious junkie...
I want all of your mind, all of your heart,
and all of your soul...
I WANT YOU!

As long as you love anything more than me....
you will NEVER be totally what I ordained for you to be...
I WEEP AT WASTE...

With that, Jesus went back to weeping.
I began to weep with Him again.
But, this time my weeping was different.
It was an elevated convicted weeping that included action,
and change within my HEART.

It was purposeful weeping.
We wept together until the sun came up the next morning.
A brand new day....

I looked for Jesus
but He had gone back to the right hand of God
to continue there, making intercession for me.

From that day forward...
I chose not to ever be the same again...
not to ever be what people wanted me to be...
but what my Lord expected me to be.

If you had seen and heard Jesus weeping...
you would know exactly what I meant...
the night Jesus wept.

The Struggle Within

Lord, I'm struggling.
My spirit and my flesh are at war.
My mind is split.
I want to do what is right.
But, what I want to do, is what I don't always do.
And what I don't want to do, I sometimes find myself
doing.
HELP ME LORD!!!!!!!!!!

Sometimes, I think it.
Sometimes, I say it.
Sometimes, I do it.
I need you Lord.

I'm struggling.
I'm sitting on this pew, struggling.
I'm sitting on this pulpit, struggling.
CHURCH as usual is not helping me.
I need someone that I can be my true self with.
I need someone to pray with me.
I need your strength.
I need to talk about it.

I don't look like what I am going through.
I'm tired of looking religious...when I'm so torn inside.

There is a storm raging within me.
The waters are surrounding me.
The clouds are hanging over me.
I'm sitting here trying to look holy, but the truth is
Lord...I'm struggling.
Everyday, I have to war against myself.
It's ME against ME!

Lord you can bring the discipline, the word, the parameters
that I am so desperately in need of.
I thank you for your Word...it is a light for my path, and a
lamp for my feet.
I praise you for your love and kindness.
There is a struggle going on in my mind Lord...
There is a storm in my heart....
And I know you are going to bring something
out of my struggle.
I know that it's going to work together for my good...

I need a Physician...

Bring peace to my spirit Lord...
Calm to my fears.
Speak to me on the deepest level of my existence.
Lead me and Guide me.

I'm going to stay on this altar of sacrifice until...
I am not going to give up.
I will never give in...
That's why I'm struggling.

I plan to fight the good fight.
I plan to keep the faith.
I plan to finish my course.

The enemy is bigger than I.
He wants to steal me, and kill me,
 and ultimately destroy me.
But I will never give up.
You are bigger than my struggle.
Your grace is sufficient.

I'm struggling in the name of the Living God.
I will be victorious.

I am more than a conqueror.
Jesus is my Help!

Woman of God...I Cover You

Woman of God,

no longer do you have to walk alone.

I have finally awaken out of my sleep.

I can see you now in the fullness of your divine essence.

I can see that I am missing a rib

...therefore I am incomplete.

I can see that you were taken out of me

from that place which is closest to my heart.

I can see that it is not good

that I should have dwelt alone.

I can see the Power of Love.

You have strength and wisdom

that has kept our world together

while I slept.

You have developed insight and fortitude

that will benefit the Kingdom of God.

You have grace and beauty

that could not have been developed in you...

unless you waited for me.

You have virtue and favor

because you are designed to care for and mother nations.

Speak to me...now that I can hear you.

Teach me...now that I can learn from you.

Follow me...now that I am following God.

Lift me...now that I understand the power you possess.

I can love you now...

because I have put away childish things..

I can love you now...

because I have become a MAN.

I can love you now...

because God has shown me how to love me.

I cannot be ME...

unless you are YOU.

Let's walk hand in hand together now.

Let's touch and agree.

Let's be fruitful and multiply our blessings as ONE.

WOMAN OF GOD...I COVER YOU.

I cover you with my spirit.

I cover you with my Manhood.

I cover you with my love.

I cover you with my essence.

I cover you with my wisdom.

I cover you with my God.

I cover you with arms of protection that will never weaken

as long as they are around you.

I waited for you to awaken me.

I waited for you as you waited for me.

I'm back at the head of the table.

I have found you.

Thanks be to God.

FIRST IT WAS MY TIME....

THEN IT WAS YOUR TIME...

NOW IT'S OUR TIME...

WOMAN OF GOD...

WOMAN OF GOD...

I mean it.

I COVER YOU.

Help Me...I Am Hurting

A woman walked into the church. She was crying as she walked directly up to the altar and laid down. She was in pain and no one seemed to know what to do.

The Altar Call had already been made and it was time for the ushers to remove her, so that the service could continue. Even the Deacons seemed agitated that she would interrupt the service like this. She wasn't even dressed for church, so why is she here, someone uttered out loud. One of the trustees went up to the pulpit and called the Pastor over and whispered in his ear...

"You have to do something about this woman, interrupting our service like this. We pay you to keep our service going so that we could get out on time....NOW DO YOUR JOB AND GET RID OF THIS WOMAN...WE VOTED YOU IN, AND WE CAN VOTE YOU OUT."

The Pastor became frightened that he would lose his income, so he motioned to his Armor-Bearer to pick the woman up and carry her out of the church, so that the announcements could be read.

One very big man, who was also a "Part-Time Bouncer at the local Strip Club...picked the woman up and she started to resist..."yelling...I need Jesus....I need Jesus.

They struggled for a moment and he over-powered her and put her on his shoulder and carried her out of the church kicking and screaming..."I need Jesus...I need Jesus!!!"

The congregation started to clap as she was removed. They couldn't believe the audacity of this woman to break into their service the way she did.

The announcements were read, and the service continued. Just before the pastor was going to get up and preach (his normal 20 minute sermon - He was only authorized by the Trustees to preach for 20 minutes or under, or they would call a meeting and straighten him out)...just as he got up, the woman ran back into the church...ran back up to the Altar and fell back down...screaming and crying...Jesus I need you...Jesus I need you!!!

This time the Deacons became irate at the fact that this woman would interrupt even the preaching.   One of the deacons ran to the Church Office and called the police...No one moved, prayed, sang, or preached until the police came.

When they got there, the deacons met them at the door. The police asked what the problem was? The deacons told them that this woman had trespassed into their church and would not leave. The Police came into the sanctuary and walked up to the Altar and told the woman that she would have to leave. The woman got up and followed the Policemen out of the church.

The Pastor then finally rose up to preach and gave his text...Luke 5:31-32 (New International Version). Jesus answered them, "It is not the healthy who need a doctor, but the sick. I have not come to call the righteous, but sinners to repentance.

His subject was..."HELP ME...I'M HURTING!"
He only had 20 minutes to deliver this message, and time was running out.

A Woman of Strength

vs.

A Strong Woman

A strong woman works out every day

to keep her body in shape...

a woman of strength kneels in prayer

to keep her soul in shape.

A strong woman is not afraid of anything...

a women of strength shows courage

in the midst of her fear.

A strong woman will not let anyone get the best of her...

a woman of strength

gives the best of her self to everyone.

A strong woman makes mistakes

and avoids the same in the future...

a woman of strength realizes that life's mistakes

can also be God's blessings

and gains strength from them.

A strong woman walks sure footedly...

a woman of strength knows God will catch her

when she falls.

A strong woman wears confidence on her face...

a woman of strength wears grace on her soul.

A strong woman has faith

that she is strong enough for the journey...

a woman of strength has faith

that it is in the journey that she will become strong.

A strong woman is present in the church every Sunday...

a woman of strength is present in the Lord everyday.

A strong woman can make it with or without a man...

a woman of strength realizes God made her for her man.

A strong woman is strong enough to get her man...

a woman of strength is strong enough to wait for her man.

A strong woman can stand alone...

a woman of strength can simply stand.

A boy can love a million girls...

but it takes a MAN to love

one WOMAN OF STRENGTH

a million ways!

Church Hurt

Church hurt is very real. What happens when the place that is suppose to provide refuge and safety for you, becomes the object of your pain?

What do you do when you have been betrayed by someone in the church who was supposed to be your brother or your sister in Christ?

Many people have left the church, vowing never to return to "that kind of fellowship." Someone once said that hurt people, hurt people.

Well if that is true, then we are all at risk of being hurt, because the churches today are full of hurt people.

Spiritual immaturity will convince you to "trust everyone in the church." So you find a brother or a sister in Christ, and you confide in them with some heavy stuff, and the next thing you know, folks are looking at you funny, and everyone knows your issues.

However, spiritual maturity will convince you to seek out the Spirit by the Spirit, and allow God to lead you to other spiritually mature people, so that they would pray with you, and for you...not harm you!

God has His children in position...those who are ready to bring healing love to hurting people, because they themselves have been through church hurt.

Woe unto to those who would intentionally and maliciously hurt one of God's children. Church is not supposed to hurt, church is supposed to heal! Too many of God's children have been hurt by the children of the devil...in the church! Too many of God's children have been scattered by wolves, who masquerade as sheep. Wolves, who are waiting to hurt and to harm you...destroy you...even kill you!

David said, "My hurt was caused by the very people who were supposed to be my family, who ate at my table, who walked and enjoyed the fellowship of my inner circle. I could have dealt with it better had it been one of my known enemies"…but this happened in the church!

What do you do…when you have experienced church hurt? Allow the peace that is within you to carry you through seasons of hurt. Walk in the knowledge that God has a plan for your life, a plan to prosper you, and not to harm you. Bring your hurt and lay it at the feet of Jesus…give it all to Him who is a healer, and a restorer. Continue to love and pray. Continue to sing and praise. Continue to hope and grow. When it's the church who has hurt you…always remember, that God knows, and He cares. So, keep the faith in God, not man and not even the church!

I'm a Woman and I'm Anointed

Many Christian women today are dealing with being accepted as equal counterparts in the ministry. There is still a holdover school of thought that believes that women should not preach, be in any leadership positions over men and even that they should keep silent in the churches and not speak or teach at all.

Now mind you, I am very much aware of what Paul wrote concerning this issue. But, I want to address, what a woman should do when she is powerfully anointed for ministry, yet still desires to remain submissive to her man as God mandates.

Paul tells us that all the members of the body are needed and that "the parts of the body that seem to be weaker are indispensable, and on those parts of the body that we think less honorable we bestow the greater honor" (1 Corinthians 12:22–23). And Jesus said, "Whoever would be great among you must be your servant" (Mark 10:43).

These statements remind us that when we talk about levels of governing authority, or levels of Bible teaching responsibility, or levels of public recognition, we are not talking about greatness or importance.

Some may question the validity of women pastors or pastor-teachers, but it must be remembered that these are gifts and not offices. Surely, women who pastor-shepherd among women should cause no problem at all (Titus 2:3–4). But in fact, Priscilla, along with Aquila, taught Apollos the way of God more accurately (Acts 18:25–26) which would indicate that a woman may not be limited to "teaching only women," nor should women be.

If God is indeed pouring out of His Spirit, onto all flesh in these days, then it is impossible for a person, male or female, to deny this outpouring and avoid it. Women must embrace this latter day move of God, knowing that God, who has begun this work in you, will complete it according to His mighty working power.

An even greater woman of God, is one who can remain powerfully anointed for God and allow the Spirit to use her, yet remain covered by her God-ordained man. She does not feel the need to usurp any authority given to the man, yet she can not and will not deny the powerful calling that is on her life.

Unfortunately, many called women of God, have responded to this gender discrimination in the church, by participating in "male-bashing," and have even become bitter towards men, but this is not the proper response. The proper response is to humbly continue in the work of the ministry, and become knowledgeable of and follow biblical guidelines on Godly submission. Remember, woman of God, you do not have to defend your ministry, or anointing to anyone. It is God who has called you, and poured out His Spirit on and in you. Spend you energy in bearing much fruit for the Kingdom, and leave the debate to God!

You can be a woman of God, and powerfully anointed, yet divinely submissive. Women who have found this righteous balance, are happiest, more complete and fulfilled. God is pleased to call you His daughter, and I am pleased to call you "one who labors beside me."

Lust or Love?

I think at some point and time in a relationship we have all had to examine our true feelings and ask ourselves if we were in lust or in love. There is a definite difference, right? Yes. No. Even... maybe so? Well the problem is by the time we find out, we are in deep, emotions are involved and sometimes we find ourselves with the wrong person. Now, that is where it gets complicated. Allow me to provide just a little background information.

Love is the foundation of families, Godly marriages, and stable societies. Lust is a physical emotion that we act upon in the "heat of the moment." Yet few among us would fall in love with someone who did not turn us on, and that can lead to problems when one or both of you gets mixed up about the difference between love and lust.

It is possible for an affair based purely on lust to develop into a healthy relationship based on love, but it does not happen all that often. You may be better off spending your time with someone who sees and appreciates you with your clothes on. Are you really in love or is it just lust?

Lust, simply put is infatuation. It is purely physical attraction. Not a bad thing - sometime that is what we need but it's not as satisfying as love. Friendship that develops into desire for each other is Love. Infatuation is like those fast food packages, which you get in the market. It looks oh-so-delicious but has little nutritional value and so you get hungry again quickly! Love is like homegrown, homemade food... which you take care of right from the time it grows on your farm and then go all the way. You have your emotions, feelings and caring nurturing it every day.

How do you feel about your love relationship? Are you insecure? Do you have doubts or questions that you feel you would rather not ask...for it might spoil your dream romance? C'mon don't push your doubts away...you know better...are you truly genuinely happy or is it just an element of excitement?

Love is the mature acceptance of imperfection. Do you know all his/her shortcomings and still find him/her attractive emotionally, intellectually, and physically? Nobody's perfect, we are all humans, we are not God; but of course you don't have to accept everything...we are all different people with different expectations...there are a few adjustments you can make and some you simply can not! You need to be able to see and recognize the difference.

When you are truly in love, long distances do make you want to be near each other but that does not lessen your love for each other. Lust on the other hand makes you look for some other excitement in place of the one you have.

Lust lacks confidence. When he/she is away, you wonder whether he/she is cheating or not. Sometimes you even play the detective and check! Love is trust. You feel calm, secure and so sure of yourself. Both of you feel that trust and it makes you respect and love each other even more than ever.

Love grows from friendship. You are friends and then you become lovers. Lust might lead you to do things you will regret later, but remember love never will. Love makes you look and think up. It makes you want to be a better person than you are now. So, think about it...were you, or are you truly in love or was it / is it just Lust?

We must understand that Love and Lust both include making love. Here is the difference, when you are in love, you want to be with that person just as much as you did before you made love. In and out of the bed, you still want to be in that person's presence, and you show it.

When it is lust, you hardly kiss during sex, and after it is over, you wipe yourself off and be on your way. That is because what you just did with that person did not involve your heart or love, only physical performance and infatuation. Love lingers, while lust comes and goes. With lust you hardly ever truly think about the other person until you want another booty-call.

Love is all about the little things. When you are really, truly, in love, you do not feel the need to dress up for them. The most important thing is being with them. Butterflies are not usually present in love. You should not feel nervous when you really love someone. Love means you connect with them spiritually, intellectually, and emotionally. Love means differences, disagreements, and arguing (but not fighting) because who wants to be with someone who is the same as they are? You feel refreshed when you are with them, but not necessarily weak when you are away from them. If you think about them all the time, always, it is probably lust or infatuation, not love. The most important thing you should consider is, can I say 'I love you' and truly mean it?

Lust is clearly not love. Love is based on more than just physical attraction. Sure, attraction is a factor, but love goes deeper than that. Love is based on caring, friendship, commitment and trust. When you are in love it is as if you have your best most trusted friend at your side AND you feel physically attracted to them. It is the best of both worlds! Love is a shared feeling between two people who have a vested interest in one another's happiness. Love is not about jealousy. It is not about conflict. It is not about testing. Love is a positive feeling. If it is tainted by mistrust, jealousy, insecurity or spitefulness it is not really love but merely a pale copy. Love is the total surrender of your heart to another person with the security of knowing that they will treat it better than you will. Love should feel good. It should not feel bad. Love should make you want to be a better person, it should not lead you to do something self-destructive. Love is not demanding of your spirit but lifts it and makes it glow. Love is a good thing. Anything less is lust, deep friendship or attraction. So with happiness aside, the question remains, how can you tell whether you are in love?

There is no easy way to find the truth behind your feelings or the feelings of another person but there are some tell-tale signs that love is blooming (or growing deeper). If you agree with at least 7 of the following 9 statements you are probably in love:

(1) You know, because you have been told by your significant other, that your deep feelings are returned in kind.

(2) The object of your affections makes you feel special and good about yourself.

(3) If/when you feel jealous it is always fleeting; you trust your partner not to betray you or hurt your relationship.

(4) Nothing makes you feel as serene as when you and your partner are together.

(5) When you fight with your partner you usually make up within a few hours and you always agree that nothing is more important than you both being able to express your true feelings (even if they sometimes cause conflict).

(6) Your partner never asks you to choose between him/her and your loyalties to your family and friends - if you do choose him/her over them you always have a good reason and it is always YOUR decision, and your decision alone.

(7) Neither you or your partner feel the need to test the other's loyalties or feelings.

(8) You are more yourself when with your partner than you are with anybody else.

(9) If sex is part of your relationship it is by mutual desire and agreement without the slightest hint of commitment testing or persuasion.

Finally, consider the word of God, when trying to distinguish what true love really is:

If I speak in the tongues of men and of angels, but have not love, I am only a resounding gong or a clanging cymbal. If I have the gift of prophecy and can fathom all mysteries and all knowledge, and if I have a faith that can move mountains, but have not love, I am nothing. If I give all I possess to the poor and surrender my body to the flames, but have not love, I gain nothing.

Love is patient, love is kind. It does not envy, it does not boast, it is not proud. It is not rude, it is not self-seeking, it is not easily angered, it keeps no record of wrongs. Love does not delight in evil but rejoices with the truth. It always protects, always trusts, always hopes, always perseveres.

Love never fails, but where there are prophecies, they will cease; where there are tongues, they will be stilled; where there is knowledge, it will pass away. For we know in part and we prophesy in part, but when perfection comes, the imperfect disappears. When I was a child, I talked like a child, I thought like a child, I reasoned like a child. When I became a man, I put childish ways behind me. Now we see but a poor reflection as in a mirror; then we shall see face to face. Now I know in part; then I shall know fully, even as I am fully known.

And now these three remain: faith, hope and love. But the greatest of these is love. I Corinthians 13 (NIV)

Boys of Flesh to Men of God

God has blessed me with three biological sons, and numerous spiritual sons. My aim is the same with every one of them...to lead them from boys of flesh to men of God.

All men are boys before they are men. So being a boy is just as critical as being a man. It is the season of sonhood, and the lessons learned there, that determines your degree of manhood.

Boys are special creatures. They are disciples (learners). They are not men yet, but they have to learn lessons pertaining to being a man.

They have to take their defeats as well as their victories and keep going. They have to learn how to win and how to lose.

Eventually, they must realize as a boy, that you don't quench every thirst...some thirsts they will have to leave unquenched...

They must learn not to define themselves with their sexual organs, but with their heart strength. The passion within each boy must be harnessed to create godly passion and satisfaction.

As they discover girls while they are still boys ...they must realize that each girl is a queen/woman/mother waiting to happen..and she is there to appreciate, respect, and love...using that passion that God gifted them with to lift their sisters up.

They must learn to love their mothers and their sisters, so that they will be able to love the woman that God has ordained for them.

Boys need both men and women to take them from boys to men. My sons need me as their role model and mentor, and teacher, and discipliner. They need their mother, as their first nurse, the first nurturer, and as their first girlfriend.

They more importantly need me as their first father, So that I might mold them and shape them into men of God...so that they can understand how to establish and maintain that all-important relationship with their heavenly Father.

I need continued godly wisdom, to guide them through the times in which they live. Teaching them commitment, responsibility, compassion, and character. Strength, courage, and boldness...to be who they are! Praising them as princes-kings, encouraging them as men-to-be.

I watch them play, sometimes I play with them...I watch them compete, sometimes I compete with them. They are strong in their own way, and weak in their own way.

I accept both realities (strengths and weaknesses) in them, and try to teach them how to live with their whole self.

They are my sons, my boys...they will carry my legacy when I go to the Father...they will always be Murray sons.

God made me their father, and I don't take it lightly. I see myself in them all the time.

I am watching their muscles grow, and their spirit grow...their voices get heavier, and hair growing. I am watching life's lessons being presented to them. At times, I can't intervene, because of the lesson that God is trying to teach them.

They must cry sometimes, for they must know pain, they must know loss sometimes, for they must know defeat, they must know that they have faults, for they must know the awesome power of God.

There is a undeveloped king in these princes. Patience and discipline must be administered to them, so that the king will someday manifest fully within them, and make them the men that God has destined them to be.

These are my boys, my sons, my heart, my joy, my loins.

Thank you God for this awesome responsibility of raising boys to men.

Breaking up is Hard to Do

"Remember…you gave "it" to Me…
but realize that it will not be easy.

But you can bear it…it is painful…but you can bear it!
Give the *pain* to Me!

Take it one day at a time…
like today, just let it go today.

You have done all that you know how to do…
now let it go!

I will work everything out…if you let Me.

I am yet making up my mind whether you two will be one.
Remember…if I will it…it shall be!

If I do not want it for you…it should not be,
And that would mean that I have something more suitable
for you.

Try not to worry too much about it, just know that I am in
control of it.

I am working it out as you read this.
I am the Great I AM…and I will work this all out in my
time.

Do not try to fix it any longer…work on yourself at this
time with Me.

You know the issues that you and I should be working on.
You gave "it" to Me…and I want to do with them as I
please.

I want also, to do with you as I please…surrender to Me!
You cannot change this…but I can.

You can only change your behaviors.
You cannot fix this, but I can.

You and I can only fix you…
Let's do that!

All you can do, as far as "it" is concerned,
 is get in My way.

Let go and Let Me take it from here…ok?
Trust Me…Trust Me….realize that I know what I am
doing.

I am working all things out for you in my own way
 and in my own time.

Trust Me…you already gave it to Me,
so do not take it back.

It's in My hands now…
don't let the devil fool you anymore!

Take it one day at a time and work on YOU.
Be strong!

Trust that the pain that you feel will not be forever.
One day it will all be over.

I have that day already appointed.
One day I will take away this pain.

But, this is where I want you right now.

Be patient…wait on Me…I am doing something great within you right now.

Everything will be alright…whichever way things turn out. If "it" is for you…I will bring them back to you…with both of you being correct and ready.

If that is the case, then know that I am working on them and you, and it will take time.

If they are not for you…
then I will not give them back to you.

Be patient my child…wait on Me…I fix things in My own time…not yours!

I shall deliver!"

Getting to the Real Issue

I have told so many lies that I need to find my way back to the truth.

I am not sure exactly who I really am. I am lost!

I became what I needed to become in order to get what I wanted.

I am lost in a world of lies, deceit, and manipulation. I am very sick.

The problem is…that I lied to myself, I deceived myself, and I manipulated me.

The real issue is me. The problem is me.

My head…my thinking…ME!!!

I am not sure how to live…but I can't let you know that…

I am not sure how to be me….I am not sure who I am anymore.

Was I put on earth to be a dope fiend…or a drunk…or a crack-head?

Was I put on earth to be the other woman, or a fornicator?

Was I put on earth to lie, steal, and gossip.

Was I put on earth to remain jealous and envious of my brothers and sisters?

Is this all that there really is to me?

Can I find my way back to myself?

Or am I just kidding myself about changing things?

Wasting time…Again!

The real issue is me….MY SIN!!

I caused it. I did it. I lied…I stole…I cheated…and I didn't even care.

All I ever think about is me…you hurt ME…you did this to ME. ME…ME…ME…My Flesh. My needs. My wants. My appetite. My belly!

The truth is…that I am sick and tired of being ME.

I need to change…but I have never ever been able to. Sure…for a few days, or maybe even a few weeks, but I always go back.

I need to change ME. Because this ME is very sick…and somewhere deep in my soul, I want to get better. I just don't know how to get better…or how to get to that deep part. HELP ME LORD!

So I'm gonna reach out…I'm gonna take a chance…what have I got to lose?

I am already on my way to hell.

What will they put on my tombstone? Sinner? Or saved by grace?
I have got to change…I have got to uncover the _real me_?

Ok…I'm gonna open up the door to my hurts and pains, and I am gonna trust God.

I tried everything else…I might as well give this a try…HONESTY.

The real issue is ME. Have mercy on me Lord!

I am the problem. I am the one who chooses. I am the decision-maker.

It begins and ends with ME.

I am the ANSWER!!!

I am the QUESTION!!!!

I Surrender

Dear Lord…I Surrender. I am willing to receive what You give. I am willing to lack what You withhold. I am willing to relinquish what You take.   I am willing to suffer what You inflict. I am willing to be what You require

Judge Not

I was shocked, confused, bewildered
as I entered Heaven's gate,
Not by the beauty of it all,
nor the lights or my glorious fate.

But it was the people in there
who made me wonder and think--
the thieves, the liars, the sinners,
the drug addicts and them who would always drink.

There stood the kid from fourth grade
who stole my lunch money twice.
Next to him was my nasty neighbor
who never said anything nice.

Mr. Adams, who I always thought
was rotting away in hell,
was resting pretty in his mansion,
looking very well.

I whispered to Jesus, "Lord, what's the deal?
These people were a terror.
How'd all these sinners get up here?
God must've made a error.

"And why's everyone so quiet,
so somber - please give me a clue."
"Be quiet, child," He said, "they're all in shock.
No one thought they'd be seeing you."

JUDGE NOT.

Memo From God

Effective immediately, please be aware that there are changes you need to make in your life. These changes need to be completed in order that I may fulfill my promises to you, to grant you peace, joy and happiness in this life. I apologize for any inconvenience, but after all that I am doing, this seems very little to ask of you. I know, I already gave you the Ten Commandments. Keep them. But, follow these ten guidelines, also.

1. QUIT WORRYING

Life has dealt you a blow and all you do is sit and worry. Have you forgotten that I am here to take all your burdens and carry them for you? Or do you just enjoy fretting over every little thing that comes your way?

2. PUT IT ON THE LIST

Something needs to be done or to be taken care of. Put! it on the list. No, not YOUR list. Put it on MY to-do-list! . Let ME be the one to take care of the problem. I can't help you until you turn it over to me. And although my to-do-list is long, I am after all, God. I can take care of anything you put into my hands. In fact, if the truth were ever really known, I take care of a lot of things for you that you never even realize.

3. TRUST ME

Once you've given your burdens to me; quit trying to take them back. Trust in me. Have the faith that I will take care of all your needs, your problems and your trials. Problems with the kids? Put them on my list. Problem with finances? Put it on my list. Problems with your emotional roller coaster? For my sake, put it on my list. I want to help you. All you have to do is ask.

4. LEAVE IT ALONE

Don't wake up every morning and say, "Well, I'm feeling much stronger now, I think I can handle it from here." Why do you think you are feeling stronger now? It's simple. You gave me your burdens and I'm taking care of them. I also renew your strength and cover you in my peace. Don't you know that if I give you these problems back, you will be right back where you started? Leave them with me and forget about them. Just let me do my job.

5. TALK TO ME

I want you to forget a lot of things. Forget what was making you crazy. Forget the worry and the fretting because you know I'm in control. But there's one thing I pray you never forget. Please don't forget to talk to me - OFTEN I love you. I want to hear your voice. I want you to include me in on the things going on in your life. I want to hear you talk about your friends and family. Prayer is simply you having a conversation with me. I want to be your dearest friend.

6. H AVE FAITH

I see a lot of things from up here that you can't see from where you are. Have faith in me that I know what I'm doing. Trust me; you wouldn't want the view from my eyes. I will continue to care for you, watch over you, and meet your needs. You only have to trust me. Although I have a much bigger task than you, it seems as if you have so much trouble just doing your simple part. How hard can trust be?

7. LOVE THEM ANYWAY

This is how the world is going to know that you are my
disciples. By the love that you have for one another. I know
that they have talked abut you, and did you wrong. I know
that they have betrayed you, and called you everything but
a child of God. I know that you have been hurt by them..
But I command you to love them as I have loved you. I so
loved you that I gave my only begotten Son. I so loved you
that I gave my life for you. If you love them anyway, then
you and I will always have fellowship together. And don't
forget how much I forgave you.

8. SAY HALLELUJAH ANYHOW

I'm looking for worshippers and praisers who will worship
and praise me in spirit and in truth. I know that sometimes I
allow you to be cast into the valley. I also see you spending
time on the mountaintop. Sometimes I allow you to go
through valley experiences to see if you will still worship
and praise me. I have righteous thoughts that I think toward
you. Thoughts of peace and not of evil, to give you a future
and a hope. Yes, all things are working together for your
good…the valleys and the mountaintops. So you just might
as well continually say…Hallelujah anyhow!

9. PRESS ON

When things get tough and the roads gets rough. Press on.
PUSH - Pray Until Something Happens! Keep moving
forward. I will give you the strength and the wisdom to
know what to do in the midst of life. I will be like a light
that will guide you along the dark and dreary paths of this
life. Press on even when you feel defeated. Because you are
never defeated. You are victorious, because I have given
you the victory, and I will never take it back. So when your
back is against the wall…press on!

10. BE THANKFUL

Whatever you have, and whatever you don't have...just be grateful. I'm looking for an attitude of gratitude from you. I have given you my grace and my mercy. And those two things are sufficient for you. So be glad. Be thankful for another chance. Be thankful that weeping may endure for a night but joy is coming in the morning. I didn't say which morning, but joy is coming. Give thanks in all things. Show your gratitude. Being thankful will make room for you to receive more of Me.

The Beauty of Our Love

The beauty of our love is so real.
We always want to be with one another…

We still love each other.
We realized that we are not perfect and that we will all
make mistakes.

We know that it is so much better to forgive mistakes.
God gives us brand new mercies everyday because we are
all sinners.

God gave us one another, and our lives changed forever.
We both finally found a reason to open our hearts up.

We both finally found a reason to love and just be
ourselves.

But, we still needed to work on our weaknesses and our
strengths.

We both knew that God bought us together for a divine
purpose.

Now things are not like before and we are both hurting.

It is so hard to think that things may never be the same way
again.

Since the day our eyes first met, we never knew a day
without each other.

We mean so much to each other…like an apple to an apple
tree.

We pray for God to make a way for us to be again.

Reality is sometimes hard to accept when you love
someone so deeply.

We love one another deeply...
and will we ever find such a love again?

Will the Lord provide that kind of love in our hearts again?

Our names are not only written on our flesh,
they are also written on our hearts...

Both places are written with permanent ink...
it can't be washed off.

It can only be covered over by something that wasn't meant
to be there.

I don't know what else to do.
The Lord knows where our hearts are.

The Lord knows what we desire.
The Lord knows who we are....

May God show us the way.
We are *one* in our book. We are *one* in God's book.

So, I will go on as a child of God ought to.
We must continue to say our prayers at night.

We must continue to open up God's Word so that we can
feed others.

But right now we need prayers…
right now we need to be fed.

Right now we need the Lord for us….
God please help us!!!

The beauty of our love is so real.
Your name means everything to us.

The way of Christ is the way of love.
Remember true love…

because true love comes only from God.
Thank you for everything…*ONE LOVE!*

The Boy in You

Hey, I'm the boy in you...you know me!

I'm the one that makes sure that you stay a loser in life.

I'm the one that never allows you to take responsibility for anything.

I'm the one that makes sure that you never want anything real...because that's too hard.

I keep you drinking and using drugs because I make sure that you never face up to life.

I make sure that you cheat in your relationships...

I make sure that you don't go to work...

I make sure that your kids are confused and hurt.

I make sure that your pockets stay empty...

I make sure that you stay depressed and angry because you can't have your way...

I am the boy in you.

I will stay around and make sure that you never ever grow up.

I will stay around and make sure that you never become a real man...

You love me because you feed me all the time...you wanna feed me right now...right?

You love me because you are afraid to let go of me…I'm laughing at you!

You love me because you think I love you…but I hate you because you are ignorant and don't know it yet.

I will never ever let you go…boy! You are really a boy in a man's body!!!!

I'll make sure that your woman will never ever expect you to be a man…

I'll make sure that your children will never ever expect you to be a man…

And soon both your woman and your kids will be calling somebody else Daddy!

Look at where I have you right now…stuck on stupid!

I got you again…and I will get you again and again and again if you ever try to leave me…

I'm all in you…in your choices…in your decisions…in the places you go…

I will never ever let you go…remember you are a boy!

I'll make sure that you stay a boy because I don't really want you to become a man…because if you become a man, what will happen to me?

I don't want to see you grow up…you belong to me…you are me…you are a boy!

I'm gonna let you think that you are becoming a man…but you'll be back.

I will let you think that you are changing and you are trying to grow up…

That's a joke…you are only fooling yourself...again!

You know my number and you will call me as soon as life gets too hard for you.

You are nothing but a boy and you know it…face it...life's too hard for you as a man.

And, here you are trying to do a man's job…that is so ridiculously funny!

Admit it now and give this man stuff up…because being a man is man's work.

So, go and get our pacifier…our crack stem, our dirty needle, our bottle…And stop fooling yourself…you are a boy and you will always be a boy.

Let your woman, and your kids find a real man…so that they can be happy!

And let me and you go get high and forget things.

I'm the boy in you and I will never ever let you go!
Will you ever let me go????

The Cry of the Wounded

I'm really wounded...I'm hurting off of some real stuff! I've been in pain for a very long time...I've just kept it all inside...but I have to get rid of this.

I can't carry this anymore...it's killing me softly! I need help...I'm not gonna make it without some help. I'm gonna die this time...I don't have another run in me.

I'm so tired...I'm so sick and tired...I'm so sick and tired of being sick and tired...I know that I cannot do this on my own. I'm gonna die if I don't change.

I must change...I must stop this madness now...but I don't know how.

I need a "right now" blessing...this is a real turning point. Change or die...those are my only two choices left. I'm really wounded...I'm hurting off of some real stuff!

Here I am, alone deep inside of this cave of despair, and desperation...I am alone...everything, everyone is gone right now. Here I am all alone with my thoughts...I am crying inside. I am scared, hurt, confused, wounded, I am bleeding to death!

But I have a little strength left...it aint much strength! I have to be true to myself.

I've got two hands! I have a gun in one hand...and I have a prayer in my other hand...Which one do I use? Which one will get the job done? Which one?

The gun will end it all...or will it? The prayer will end it all...or will it?

The pain of not changing is greater than the pain of changing. I know that I want to live but I don't know how. Is dying easier?

Put the gun down, get on your knees and use the prayer!

How do I know that this will work? How do I know?

Prayer changes things. You don't have to stay messed up. There is a God who loves you. Hear my voice. God loves you. Yes, even you. No one has gone down so far that the love of God can't reach you. Give it to God! Use the power of prayer.

Well, it's worked for many others, and it is "the cry of the wounded!!!"

Change or Die!!!

I SURRENDER ALL!!!

My Mother

She welcomed me into her womb.

She carried me in safety to ensure my arrival to this world.

I was her child.

MY MOTHER

She had done it before,

she had given birth to her other seeds.

She is my mother.

She nourished me with her breast milk,

ensuring my growth.

She held me when I was sad,

and told me everything would be alright.

She counseled me, when I was straying from the path.

She nursed my earliest wounds and scars, hurts and pains.

She was the first object of my affection.

Before I learned to love God, I learned to love her.

She is my mother.

She taught me how to walk.

She taught me how to talk.

She taught me how to eat.

She taught me how to sleep.

She taught me how to live.

She taught me...

She tooked me to church and showed me her God...

and her God became my God!

She helped me pray when I didn't have the words.

She helped me with school work,

as she trained me to become my destiny.

She went through many rough times to ensure my survival.

She went without what she needed,

so that I could have what I needed.

She sacrificed most of her goals...

to be a good mother to all of her children.

I really don't need a calendar to tell me when to show her

my appreciation for all that she has done for me.

I live my life as a living testimony to the fact that she did her job well.

I love you mom....

YOU ARE MY MOTHER!

I thank God for you. I will take care of you now!

EVERYDAY IS MOTHER'S DAY!

Whatever Happened to the Fear of God?

The greatest problem facing man at this hour is: man has lost his fear of God.

The fear of God. radiates out from our adoration and devotion to everyday conduct that sees each moment as the Lord's time, each relationship as the Lord's opportunity, each duty as the Lord's command, and each blessing as the Lord's gift. It is a new way of looking at life and seeing what it is meant to be when viewed from God's perspective.

The fear of the Lord is just the proper reaction of sinners to God's infinite holiness, or of creatures to God's infinite majesty. As we grow in the knowledge of God, we will learn truly to tremble before His great glory and burning purity, and see this as indeed the beginning of wisdom.

The fear of God brings temporal and eternal benefits:

1. "The secret of the Lord is for those who fear Him, and He will make them know His covenant" (Psalms 25:14).

2. "The angel of the Lord encamps around those who fear Him, and rescues them" (Psalms 34:7).

3. "The Lord has compassion on those who fear Him" (Ps. 103:13).

4. "The Lord favors those who fear Him" (Ps. 147:11).

5. "The fear of the Lord is the beginning of wisdom" (Prov. 1:7; 9:10).

6. "The fear of the Lord prolongs life" (Prov. 10:27).

7. "The fear of the Lord leads to life, that one may sleep satisfied, untouched by evil" (Prov. 19:23).

8. "The reward of humility and the fear of the Lord are riches, honor and life" (Prov. 22:4).

9. As David says to the Lord, "How great is Your goodness, which You have stored up for those who fear You" (Ps. 31:19).

Clearly, fearing God is to your great advantage.

However, man seems more in fear of man than in fear of God. Yes, we stand at the crossroads between fear of others and fear of God. The road leading to the fear of man may be expressed in terms of favoritism, wanting others to think well of you, fearing exposure by them, or being overwhelmed by their perceived physical power. When these fears are not combated with the fear of the Lord, the consequences can be devastating. But when God is given his rightful place in our lives, old bonds can be shattered. We are more concerned about looking stupid (a fear of people) than we are about acting sinfully (fear of the Lord).

We fear men so much, because we fear God so little. One fear cures another. When man's terror scares you, turn your thoughts to the wrath of God

.

On one side, the fear of the Lord does indeed mean a terror of God (threat-fear). We are unclean people, and we appear before the Almighty God who is morally pure. We are rightly ashamed before Him, and punishment would be completely just... But at the other end...is a fear reserved exclusively for those who have put their faith in Jesus Christ. This fear of the Lord means reverent submission that leads to obedience, and it is interchangeable with "worship," "rely on ," "trust," and "hope in." Like terror, it includes a knowledge of our sinfulness and God's moral purity, and it includes a clear-eyed knowledge of God's justice and his anger against sin. But this worship-fear also knows God's great forgiveness, mercy, and love. It knows that because God's eternal plan, Jesus humbled himself by dying on a cross to redeem his enemies from slavery and death. It knows that, in our relationship with God, he always says "I love you" first. This knowledge draws us closer to God rather than causing us to flee. It causes us to submit gladly to His lordship and delight in obedience. This kind of robust fear is the pinnacle of our response to God.

This is one of the great blessings of the fear of the Lord. We think less often about ourselves. When a heart is being filled with the greatness of God, there is less room for the question, "What are people going to think of me?"

What exactly is this fear of God? It is the non-negotiable motivator of the believer. God, His presence, His will, and His glory are the reason the believer does what he does. He has a single motivation in his life – to live so as to please his Lord. He does not live for his own pleasure or the pleasure of others. He does not live for what he can possess. He does what he does because God is and has spoken. This is the sole guidance system for his existence. He does what he does not because someone is watching, or out of fear of the consequences, but ultimately because of a deep, worshipful love and reverence for God. The thought of knowingly and purposefully disobeying Him is unthinkable.

To fear God means that my life is structured by a sense of awe, worship, and obedience that flows out of recognizing Him and His glory. He becomes the single most important reference point for all that I desire, think, do, and say. God is my motive and God is my goal. The fear of God is meant to be the central organizing force in my life.

Fearing God has two aspects. The first is reverence. It is a sacred awe of God's utter holiness. It involves the kind of respect and veneration that results in fear in the presence of such absolute majesty. The second aspect is fear of God's displeasure. Genuine faith acknowledges God's right to chasten, His right to punish, and His right to judge.

The fear of the Lord tends to take away all other fears. This is the secret of Christian courage and boldness. I fear God, and therefore there is none else that I need fear.

There is a true sense in which you must teach your children to fear God, and especially to fear His displeasure. You have not satisfied the responsibilities of parenthood when you have made your child submit to you. If you are consistent and firm in your discipline, your child may obey you because he or she fears violating your standards. That is a fairly easy thing to achieve. But it is not the proper goal of biblical parenting. Your child should fear violating God's standard, not merely yours. You are only an intermediary with the responsibility of teaching your child to fear God. If your children grow up fearing only your displeasure but not God's, what will they do when you are not there?

To fear the Lord is to tremble at the thought of offending him by unbelief and disobedience. It is the feeling that God is not to be played with. Believers are described as fearing the name of God; we should be reverent worshippers; we should stand in awe of the Lord's authority; we should be afraid of offending Him; we should feel their own nothingness in the sight of the Infinite One. Again, the Lord favors those who fear him.

When Men Pray Together

When men pray together...the earth trembles and shakes.
When men pray together...the family strengthens.
When men pray together...the women look on, in satisfied
and aroused amazement.

You see there is something so special about seeing men
pray together. It makes you feel safe and secure.
It makes the world more understandable and tolerable.

When men pray together, God smiles from heaven and
beats his chest, in proud satisfaction. God is pleased when
men pray together...He thinks "wow, they are finally
getting it!"

Men praying together is a powerful statement of pure
spiritual force gathering like a rushing mighty wind.
A wind so strong it can defeat anything that stands in it's
path, and it swirls up to the highest mountain and declares
its unstoppable directive.

Men praying together means, the women are safe...it means
the children are fed...it means the earth is at peace...it
means God has been given His rightful place in our soulful
existence.

The power of prayer is undeniable.
The power of men is God-given.
The power of togetherness is wisdom-based.

I'm longing to pray with my brothers...
I'm longing for me and my brothers, both young and old,
fathers and sons...to come together and pray for our
women, our children, our communities, our relationship
with our God, our homes, our combined and joined

destinies...I LONG FOR THIS!!!

This will make us deeper men of God...stronger fathers...anointed heads and priests in our homes...righteous leaders in our communities...POWERFUL TRUE MANHOOD ON DISPLAY for the devil to tremble at the very thought and pure sound of men praying together!

There is only one thing more powerful than men praying together. That is...a man, his woman and his children praying together!

Love Power

"No one falls in love by choice; it is by CHANCE
(Purpose).
No one stays in love by chance; it is by WORK
(Prayer).
And no one falls out of love by chance; it is by CHOICE
(Neglect)."

Holding on and hanging in there may not necessarily be
signs of great strength.

However there are times when it takes much more strength
to know when to let go and then do it. They apply to both
Love and Life.

To My Friends Who Are MARRIED
Love is not about "It's your fault", but "I'm sorry."
Not "Where are you?", but " I'm right here."
Not "How could you?", but "I understand."
Not "I wish you were", but "I'm thankful you are."

To My Friends Who Are SINGLE
Love is like a butterfly.
The more you chase it, the more it eludes you.
But, if you just let it fly, it will come to you
when you least expect it.

Love can make you happy
but often it hurts,
but love's only special
when you give it to someone
who is really worth it.

So take your time and choose the best.
(Men can chase, women can choose,
but neither one has to look for it.
It grows while you're not looking.)

To My Friends Who Are NOT SO SINGLE
Love isn't about becoming somebody else's "perfect
person". It's about finding someone who
helps you become the best person you can be.

To My Friends Who Are PLAYBOY/GIRL TYPE
Never say "I love you" if you don't care.
Never talk about feelings
if they aren't there.

Never touch a life
if you mean to break a heart.
Never look in the eye when all you do is lie.
The cruelest thing a guy can
do to a girl is to let her fall in love
when he doesn't intend to catch her fall
and it works both ways.

To My Friends Who Are ENGAGED
The true measure of compatibility is not the years
spent together, but how good you are for each other.

To My Friends Who Are HEARTBROKEN
Heartbreaks last as long as you want
and cut as deep as you allow them to go.
The challenge is not how to survive heartbreaks
but to learn from them.

To My Friends Who Are NAIVE

How to be in love: Fall but don't stumble, be consistent but not too persistent, share and never be unfair, understand and try not to demand, and get hurt but never keep the pain.

To My Friends Who Are POSSESSIVE
It breaks your heart to see the one you love happy with
someone else
but it's more painful to know
that the one you love is unhappy with you.

To My Friends Who Are AFRAID TO CONFESS
Love hurts when you break up with someone.
It hurts even more when
someone breaks up with you.
But love hurts the most
when the person
you love has no idea how you feel.

To My Friends Who Are STILL HOLDING ON
A sad thing about life is when you meet someone and fall
in love, only to find out in the end that it was never meant
to be and that you have wasted years on someone who
wasn't worth it. If he isn't worth it now ' he's not going to be
worth it a year or 10 years from now.
Let it go.....

TO ALL MY FRIENDS...
My wish for you is a man/woman whose love is honest,
strong, mature, never-changing, uplifting, protective,
encouraging, rewarding and unselfish.

My Father and Me

My father was a great man because he was MY father. The only one I ever had.

He had faults, but I know he loved me. I have faults too.

I know times were not always easy for you Dad. You grew up on a Share Cropper's Farm in South Carolina, and you never got to go to school.

You and Mom didn't make it together, but I know you loved her. You tried your best to make me feel like a son.

You never took a lesson on how to be a Dad, but yet you were my Dad...the only one I ever had. God didn't make a mistake by making me your son. I know I have a lot of you in me, Mom told me that.

There were times when you hit Mom, and I didn't like that. You should not have put your hands on her. I have learned that I am to never hit a woman, and I learned that from you, because when you would hit Mom, I saw the great pain it caused her, inside and outside.

I love you Dad, because you are MY Dad. I never really got to know you man to man, because God took you before I was spiritually mature enough to approach you as a man myself. I'm hindered to some degree in life because I became a man without you. But, I did become a man. Sometimes, I wanted you to be there, like when I achieve things, and when I competed in sports...or when I preach. I want to look out and see MY father. But God is my Father too, and He teaches me what
I need to know.

So it's Father's Day again Dad, and you're not here with me physically. I never really had you here with me physically. But I honor you on Father's Day. I honor your Fatherhood and your love for me, your son.

You have never known me as a Minister of the Gospel, you have never seen me Preach the Word of God, you have never sat in a pew of a church that I pastored, because God took you before all of that happened. But I'm happy that you were my Dad. And I'm not Father less. Well, I'm a Father now too...I have three sons of my own, Gregg, Jr., Joshua, and Jeremiah. I'm teaching them how to be men of God. Just like you taught me. I've learn from the things you did and the things you didn't do. I hug them often, because you never hugged me, and by not having that, I learned the importance of hugging my children, especially my sons.

I have to go now Dad...rest in peace! People ask me sometimes about where my father is...and I smile because, I know that my father is in me, and I am in him. You are, and you forever will be...MY FATHER!

What is the Biblical Role and Duties of a Pastor's Wife

The Bible does not address the involvement of the pastor's wife in any ministry. In other words, it depends upon the denomination, the individual church within a denomination, the church board, and the pastor and his wife to determine how active the pastor's wife should be. The main area of responsibility for any wife is to support and be submissive to her husband (Ephesians 5:22-24). However, if the Lord calls a man into the ministry, He calls the whole man, and that includes the man's wife and his family.

The Apostle Paul in 1 Timothy 3 gives us the qualifications of a "bishop" or what we call a pastor, and in verse 4 we see the following: "one who rules his own house well, having his children in submission with all reverence." "Rules well" is an idiom for being a biblical husband with a submissive wife and children that love and respect him. The pastor who is the head of his home will be more successful as a leader in the church, and of course, this means that his wife is his helper in the ministry of the home as well as the church. The ministry is a partnership in all areas of life and not just in the home life.

The wife does not do the work of the pastor, but the pastor and his wife are a team who are yoked together to do God's work. Too few recognize the reality of this and want to put the pastor's wife in a box and relegate her to keeping the home fires burning and prayer support for her husband. That certainly is her responsibility, but quite often, the pastor's wife has gifts that can and should be used in the ministry. On the other hand, there are women whose husbands are pastors and they see it as "his" ministry and do not enter in to the work in any way. There should be a good balance between these two ideas with the goal of bringing glory to God in all things. An active, outgoing pastor's wife is a valuable asset to any church in today's climate of apathy to the things of God.

She should fully support her husband's ministry and not do him any harm. She might have to keep things just between her and God. She would have to understand that she must share the man of God with his flock. But, she must also understand how much he needs her to be what no other member of his flock could be. The wife has to be called to be a pastor's wife. She must see it as her ministry, and take it as serious as the church serving Jesus Christ. She must know his weaknesses, and apply strength and encouragement there.

The pastor's wife must be the closest human being to the pastor and his heart. She can make him or break him! Choose wisely.

Posts on the Wall

- *Stop lying on God! God did not send you a married person....satan did! You're confused because it feels right. Feeling right don't make it right. The word of God makes it right. I'm just saying what needs to be said!*

- *Ask yourself why, and ask yourself why not, Think about what is, and then wonder about what if. Find something truly fascinating about where you are and who you are. You will find a new, effective pathway to wherever you wish to go and say yes I can and yes I will! You can do ALL things through Christ who gives you strength!*

- *When you can't control it... that is when you give it to God. When you can't move it, then let God move it. In God, being still is movement. God sends you the uncontrollable and unmovable so that He can be your control and your move. Move your control!*

- *God prefers your obedience rather than your money*

- *God loves you...and He's not two-faced!*

- *Do not let how some people see you, be the way you see yourself. You are not what they see or say. You are what God sees and says. So tell us...what are you?*

- *It is not right to break someone's heart one piece at a time. If you must break someone's heart with the truth...do it all at once. Let them have it all, and hurt one time and begin the un-interrupted healing process, rather than you keep breaking it step by step, and they have hurt on top of hurt. Remember what comes around, goes around!*

- *Silence can also be a sin.*

- *Has anyone ever considered that satan is cursing many ministries with great facilities, huge budgets and t.v. costs, so that the church will have to make raising money a bigger issue than raising souls? How about pitching a tent on a vacant lot and preaching heaven down to repentive hearts, and truly converting souls to Christ?*

- *YOU have been convinced that you deserve God's best for you. The relationships you get into will be according to what you are convinced you can have.*

- *"NEVER" is a very tricky word.*

- *Never give yourself to someone who doesn't have the spiritual capacity nor the desire to receive and return your love. Be careful who you love. Place spiritual discernment around your heart or get used to crying yourself to sleep and spending years in wasted misery.*

- *God knows the desires of your heart...but so does satan!*

- *What's driving you will determine your destination.*

- *I believe in the sun even if it isn't shining. I believe in love even when I am alone. I believe in rain even when the sun is shining and I believe God even when He is silent.*

- *Some churches are traditional funeral homes. Some are gay clubs. Some are mega Hollywood sets. Some are religious talent, modeling and fashion shows. Some are civil-war zones. Some are get rich or die trying slaughter houses. While a "remnant-few" are a chosen, holy and called out royal priesthood.*

- *Satan has unleashed a spirit of homosexuality into the atmosphere that is ordered to target children and young teenagers. Pray people of God...pray now!*

- *The church has an ongoing adulterous affair with the world. The church became pregnant and gave birth. They named the child " Prosperity Gospel"!*

- *Right now, the church is doing more talking than walking, more sinning than winning, more playing than praying, more singing than bringing, more lying than dying, more dressing than blessing, and more gossip than worship. It is time to get right church! God is watching everything!*

- *Watch who you kiss...or who you allow to kiss you.*

- *God has a plan. God is up to something. The things that are happening to you is all part of God's plan. Give God control over your life and your mind. Live for Him and trust Him. Then all will work together for your good.*

- *Do not waste time trying to change the things that you CAN'T change. Rather, spend your time changing the things that you CAN change. Ask God* to show you the difference between your Can't(s) and your Can(s). You will rest better at night!

- *The greatest and most important title I have is "Dad"!*

- *A father has to be more than a child support check!*

- *If you think only with your eyes, you will be easily fooled.*

- *Misery loves company, and his best friend is "self-centeredness"!*

- *The most selfish thing a married person could do is commit adultery.*

- *Here, then is the real problem of our negligence. We fail in our duty to study God's Word not so much because it is difficult to understand, not so much because it is dull and boring, but because it is work. Our problem is not a lack of intelligence or lack of passion. Our problem is that we are lazy.*

- *If you are cheating on your love one, love them enough to admit it and get help. Or, love them enough to walk away and stop putting them in harm's way. How can you say you love them and sleep with them, and sleep with someone else, bringing harm home to them? They deserve to be in a true Godly relationship, and so do you.*

- *At least be truthful with God and yourself.*

- *God doesn't promise us that He will always remove the storm, but He does promise us that He will be with us in the midst of the storm!*

- *Life is easier when we know what we don't know. Life is more difficult when we don't know what we don't know. Life is impossible when we don't want to know what we don't know because we think we already know it.*

- *You cannot do God's work according to the world's rules.*

- *Too many of us are taking "fornicative test drives" before marital commitments. Sex is God's wedding gift to married couples. It is not the world's way, but it's God's way. Allowing the Holy Ghost into the marriage bed will ensure compatibility in all areas.*

- *One of satan's greatest tricks is to make us feel comfortable in our sin!*

- *It takes the courage and strength of a true warrior to ask for help.*

- *There is power in forgiveness!*

- *You have to constantly remind yourself of how ignorant people can be and act. Then you will not be totally hurt or surprised by manifested ignorance.*

- *Because you are perfect, it is not easy being your friend!*

- *Sometimes, the move of God is not a move at all. Sometimes, it is simply the substance of things hoped for, and the evidence of things not seen. God is moving even when He is not moving. That is where our faith comes in and gives us a praise!*

- *A self-proclaimed perfect man is a liar!*

- *Speak those things that have not happened yet, as though they have already happened and watch God make it happen. Folks may think you have lost your mind. Tell them, you have, and you are now operating with the mind of Christ Jesus, and God said..."It is already done"!*

- *You and God can do it together! God does allow partnerships, even though He does not really need them.*

- *A woman was standing at the bus stop waiting on her bus to come. Her bus did not come when she thought it would. So, she foolishly decided to get on the very next bus that came. She ended up lost for a long time. But, her bus was so appointed, that it found her and carried her home! Do not settle. Wait on YOUR bus!*

- *Be encouraged, and do not ever give up on God. It is not over until God says it is over! Ask Lazarus and his two sisters, Mary and Martha. It is just a set up for a show up and a show out!*

- *If God can look beyond our faults and see our needs, why can't we do the same thing for one another?*

- *Much of that which physically attacks the majority of Christians could be prevented, not at the altar, but with a healthier diet and regular exercise. It is not always satan, most times, it is what is on your plate!*

- *Your walk speaks louder than your title!*

- *"Only Lady" not "First lady!"*

- *A wife who gladly submits to her godly husband is a fulfilled, joyous soul, but a wife who kills her godly husband is an empty, tormented soul.*

- *Leaving that desolate place does not mean you are leaving God. Many folks are suffering from malnutrition needlessly because they are in the wrong church! It is your fault if you die of starvation because you refuse to leave a restaurant that has run out of food!*

- *The reason why you have been feeling so out of place lately and nothing seems to fit and people close to you are acting strange, is because God is sending you somewhere. He is preparing you and easing you away from that which has been familiar to unseen areas and levels. Do not think it strange, just move with God...and do not forget to praise your way "there"!*

- *Walk like you're on your way to that place. Walk by faith, that you will reach your destination. Keep your head up so that you can see where you are going. Glance at the rear view every now and then only to see where God has brought you from. But, keep a steady pace toward the prize. Travel light...lose the unnecessary weight. It is right around the bend. PUSH!*

- *Some days, it will just be you and the Lord!*

- *When God gets ready to take you to a whole new level...expect the haters to come out in full force. Measure your anointing and purpose in God by the amount of haters you have! Remember that if God be for you...who can be against you? The weapons of " haterade" may form, but they won't prosper!*

- *Trying to please everyone is a very unfruitful way of life that you can never be successful at. So why attempt something that has a guaranteed 100% failure rate? It will leave you wasted!*

- *There is no difference between a false prophet and a fortune cookie!*

- *Some folks are so smart, that they are actually stupid! Give them time, it will come straight from their brain, right out of their mouth, without being screened by thought!*

- *What people think about you is really none of your business!*

- *Don't be so deep that you can't reach anyone but yourself!*
- *There are some things that God won't fix in a person's life, because even when it was working, it wasn't right!*

- *One very important thing to understand when making changes, is that the world or the people in it won't necessarily be changing with you.*

- *Sometimes the storms of life are raging in such an overwhelming way that we simply have to thank God that we have not lost our mind. Yes, sometimes...the blessing and the peace in the midst of the storm is...that through it all, you are still in your right mind!*

- *The key to being able to love everyone is...staying out of folks business!*

- *There is a holy rebellion currently going on in the spirit realm. God has positioned a remnant of "souled out vessels" throughout the earth, to quietly and effectively penetrate the forces of evil that are currently running most churches, in order to set the captives free. In 2010, there will be a great release of these...vessels. Satan will not be able to preen them with business as usual.*

- *My enemies only make me stronger in God.*

- *The greatest problem with the church today is not homosexuality...it is not the Prosperity Gospel...it is not because folks are not tithing... it is not sexual immorality. The greatest problem with the church today is most people are not getting converted to the Gospel of Jesus Christ. We have too much marketing and not enough salvation! It is not about true deliverance anymore, just deadly entertainment.*

- *Some have made life changing, even fatal mistakes by listening to other people and not listening to God. What you have to do will not always be understood by everyone (even you).*

- *Great things are birthed through great pain. Just ask any mother.*

- *Your best friends are not always your best friends. Be careful what you tell people.*

- *This is my position concerning women in ministry leadership positions...try to stop them and get run over! They are pastors, apostles, prophets, evangelists and teachers, and I love all of them! They are here to stay. Thank you Jesus!*

- *Today was made for you. Brand new mercies are yours for the taking. You and God can't fail as ONE. Rise to the occasion. It's yours! It's already done. Walk into your season.*

- **When the wife has her own vision, and the husband has his own vision, that's di-vision.**

- *In accordance with Proverbs 18:22...a woman who desires to be a wife must be "findable."*

- *Women if you want that man to want you, show him Christ instead of cleavage. What you draw him with, is what you are going to have to keep him with.*

- *People are dying, suffering, losing their souls and going to hell everyday. The so-called church leaders are all about money, property, power, and prestige. These things have diverted many from their primary purpose. Repent, for judgement is coming to your house!*

- *Morning Dew: Today was made for you. Brand new mercies are yours for the taking. You and God can not fail as ONE. Rise to the occasion. It is yours! It is already done. Walk into your season.*

- *Medical doctors do not have the final say...God does!*

- *The greatest obstacle to overcome in life is overcoming yourself.*

- *Many people are suffering from self-unforgiveness. You have not been able to forgive yourself for some mistake that you might have made. You are heavy-laden with guilt and shame, and that has kept you back from walking in your true purpose. Let this be the day you will forgive yourself as God has already forgiven you.*

- *If you ask for the truth...be prepared for it! It could hurt, but it always makes you free, if you allow it to. Some cannot walk in the light, because they refuse to walk in the truth!*

- *Your battles have created the warrior in you. The enemy thought they would weaken you, but they only made you stronger. Your armor may be dented, but still holding. Fight on soldier of the Most High...fight on! You do not even look like what you been through!*

- *Don't you give up! We're going to make it...with Jesus on our side, things will work out fine!*

- *The stress caused by the issues of life can create stress in your physical body. Now is the time to deal with the issues and to tie up loose ends that keep you from maintaining peace emotionally, mentally and physically. Do not delay in taking care of these matters; procrastination is your enemy. Be diligent to methodically and consistently keep moving towards freedom and tranquility.*

- *It doesn't matter how DARK the SKY, how DISCOURAGING the CIRCUMSTANCES or how DESPARATE the SITUATION God is THERE—a God who is too QUICK to FORGET and too GOOD TO FAIL. God is there! His mighty ARM ruling this universe redeeming all who will let HIM, and reinforcing all who will respond to Him in FAITH, TRUST and OBEDIENCE.*

- *Sometimes the true enemy is a "frienemy" (friendly enemy). They are the worst kind because they can "smile and stab" at the same time!*

- *Why would a pastor allow a known homosexual male or male whoremonger to preach or sit in his pulpit, but not allow an anointed woman of God in his pulpit? Some have truly lost their way.*

- *Worry is faith in the negative; trust in the unpleasant assurance of disaster and belief in defeat. Worry is wasting today's time to clutter up tomorrow's opportunities with yesterday's troubles. Worry is the sin of distrusting the promise and providence of God, and yet it is a sin that Christians commit perhaps more frequently than any other.*

- *Where is your faith? God will never leave you nor forsake you. You do not have anymore "bad" days, you only have "good" days and "necessary" days.*

- *Many Christian leaders today can not distinguish sin from the sinner and condemn both rather than reaching out to help the person and looking beyond their sin and see their need and sharing the forgiveness of God.*

- *If you give up, then you are playing right into your enemy's hand. Get up, shake yourself, dust yourself off and show them that, If God be for you, then who can be against you? You have just as much right to be happy as anybody else.*

- *Do something nice to somebody that you know does not like you and see what happens.*

- *Every time the devil reminds you of your past, remind him of his future.*

- *For a long time now, you have been struggling with something that you just can't seem to gain the upper hand on. You have placed it before God, and He doesn't seem to be willing to give you the strength to overcome it. You are pressing on with it, but it bothers you, because it surfaces every now and then. Don't worry, God's grace is sufficient. Pack that thorn up and bring it along on the journey!*

- *Position yourself for further breakthrough in your circumstances. You have been waiting for certain resolution before you can feel free to move on, and now is the time for things to get settled at least in some ways. A complete breakthrough is still ahead and will require determination to push through. But, for now you can breathe a temporary sigh of relief, says the Lord, as you gain important intermediate ground.*

- *You will only get to know God, as much as your faith allows you to.*

- *Never judge a book by only reading the last chapter, unless you love to assume things.*

- *It's up to men of God, to teach boys of God, how to treat girls of God, to become their women of God!*

- *Love is a fire. It could warm your home up, or it could burn your house down.*

- *You don't tell the truth to be accepted. You tell the truth to be set free.*

- *Be true to yourself and to God, and be less concerned with what others think about you. Don't accept their definition of you, Don't even accept your own definition of yourself, if it doesn't line up with what God says about you. Continue to grow into God's definition of you.*

- *A good Pastor hardly ever will tell you what to do. He simply oversees an atmosphere that will enable you too see it for yourself.*

- *A foolish person allows someone else to do his thinking for him; while a wise person thinks for himself, but, a Believer has the mind of Christ.*

Published by Parablist Publishing House

P.O. Box 43379
Richmond Heights, OH 44143

www.parablistpublishinghouse.com

For Speaking Engagements Contact

Dr. G. Gregg Murray at:

Website: www.ggreggmurrayministries.com

Facebook: facebook/ggmurray

Email: pastorggmurray@gmail.com

.

Made in United States
Orlando, FL
09 June 2022

18637178R00075